DEFENSIO CIVIUM:

APPARATUS FOR SECOND AMENDMENT APOLOGETICS

I0407856

By: D.A. Morse

PROLOGUE

WE THE PEOPLE. These three words are perhaps the most paramount within the first paragraph of the Constitution of the United States of America. It establishes by whom this great country will be run. The People, not the government, are the true governors of this country. However, We the People have forgotten such a crucial detail. We the People have willingly forfeited our sovereignty to those who we deem themselves more capable. Unfortunately, over the years, we have been continuously beaten down by the same. Modern politicians, like kings, do not care for the rights of the common citizens, only their money. Their concerns lie with their legacy, their kingdom. Their kingdom consists of their own self-interests, not the interests of We the People.

Fortunately for the common American citizen, our Founding Fathers foresaw this form of despotism. We are all familiar with these words etched in the Declaration of Independence:

That whenever any Form of Government becomes destructive of these ends, it is the Right of the People to alter or to abolish it, and to institute new Government, laying its foundation on such principles and organizing its powers in such form, as to them shall seem most likely to effect their Safety and Happiness...

...But when a long train of abuses and usurpations, pursuing invariably the same Object evinces a design to reduce them under absolute Despotism, it is their right, it is their duty, to throw off such Government, and to provide new Guards for their future security.

These two segments establish the understanding that the People, not the government, are ultimately responsible for their future. However, there is another, unfamiliar, segment which connects these two phrases.

...Prudence, indeed, will dictate that Governments long established should not be changed for light and transient causes; and accordingly all experience hath shewn, that mankind are more disposed to suffer, while evils are sufferable, than to right themselves by abolishing the forms to which they are accustomed...

This is the current state of our nation. We have become accustomed to the corruption. We are disposed to suffer and to suffer the evils of the politicians. And worse, We the People have decided not only to accept the corruption of government, but are gradually giving up the means of throwing off such corruption and to re-establish the sovereignty of the People. The means in question is our right to keep and bear arms.

We, as a nation, have allowed politicians to decide what sort of "reasonable" gun legislation should be instituted. We have failed to educate those who would be beguiled by the euphemisms strategically employed by politicians who prefer an unarmed populace. The common citizen listens to the uninformed and deceitful politicians or the media's talking heads spewing inaccuracies or emotional drama from their television screens, computer monitors, and other handheld devices. The media is saturated by misinformation designed to confuse or bewilder the common citizen into believing they are incapable of controlling a firearm or have no chance to defend themselves from evil, no matter what form that evil may take. And many have believed this drivel, this condescending lecture, toward the peasants from the nobles.

Yet, there are many still who understand, at least at some level. the importance of "We the People" and the "Common Defence". These citizens resolve to take responsibility over their future and their lives in the present. They are a dying breed. Too many young men and women are relinquishing their independence for a false sense of security supposedly provided by our government.

Scandal after political scandal has determined this is untrue. We have recently confirmed, I say confirmed since there has been a long lasting suspicion, our government will repeatedly violate the Constitution, the very document designed by and for We the People, for their own personal gain and enrichment. With every tragic loss of life committed by a criminal or terrorist, the lies pour forth from the media concerning the intent of the Second Amendment, firearms, and their owners. As a result, our freedoms have been slowly diminished. So slowly in fact, the People have hardly noticed until of late.

The question now is what shall we do? We are in a strange time in our country's history. We have again become divided for reasons which should have died long ago. We are not at the point to cast off our government, nor have we hit the point of a second civil war, but the tensions seem to be rising with each new president. The unfortunate prediction of George Washington is coming to pass:

The alternate domination of one faction over another, sharpened by the spirit of revenge, natural to party dissension, which in different ages and countries has perpetrated the most horrid enormities, is itself a frightful despotism. But this leads at length to a more formal and permanent despotism. The disorders and miseries which result gradually incline the minds of men to seek security and repose in the absolute power of an individual; and sooner or later the chief of some prevailing faction, more able or more fortunate than his competitors, turns this disposition to the purposes of his own elevation, on the ruins of public liberty.
- George Washington, Farewell Address, 1796[1]

This prediction is the line which must be crossed. For now, we wait. However, we must continue the fight to defend the most paramount of rights with which each and every citizen is born, the right to keep and bear arms. This is the fundamental measure which the Founders of this country established for future generations to use as a tool to form and shape our freedom. The Second Amendment is the leverage the People of the United States maintain to keep those who would transform the representation entrusted to them into power over them. It is our shield and sword against tyranny and those that prey on the good and decent citizens. Without it, we are always but a single politician away from a dictatorship. To give up this right would mean ruin for our Republic and the extinction of the freedoms we the People enjoy. For this reason, the purpose of this booklet is to offer the common citizen the knowledge to defend the Second Amendment and our basic right to self-defense.

This booklet shall serve as a tool of combat on the battlefield of ideas regarding the gun debate. My hope is other common citizens such as myself will gain the knowledge needed not only to defend the Second Amendment, but the Constitution as a whole.

---

[1] Washington, George. "Farewell Address." 1796. *Ourdocuments.gov*. Web. 24 Mar. 2017. <https://www.ourdocuments.gov/doc.php?doc=15&page=transcript>.

PART I
Why a Second Amendment?

As declared in the preamble of the Constitution of the United States, one of the provisions of the document is "for the Common Defence". This Common Defence appears first in the form of the Article I, Section 8, Clause 12-15 which reads:

To raise and support armies, but no appropriation of money to that use shall be for a longer term than two years;

To provide and maintain a navy;

To make rules for the government and regulation of the land and naval forces;

To provide for calling forth the militia to execute the laws of the union, suppress insurrections and repel invasions;

To provide for organizing, arming, and disciplining, the militia, and for governing such part of them as may be employed in the service of the United States, reserving to the states respectively, the appointment of the officers, and the authority of training the militia according to the discipline prescribed by Congress;

However, this section concerned several representatives during and following the ratification process. Even though the Clause 15 states that Congress has power to provide the militia the means of fighting, it did not guarantee that the citizens that make up the militia could arm themselves. Many representatives feared that giving the government the power to retain the means by which the militia could cast off another tyranny, the government could and would easily return to such a form. Furthermore, several representatives were apprehensive about a standing army in general. These concerns can be seen in their arguments:

"My great objection to this government is, that it does not leave us the means of defending our rights, or of waging wars against tyrants."
   - *Patrick Henry (Elliot's Debates, 3:47; in Virginia Ratifying Convention)[2]*

"What, Sir, is the use of a militia? It is to prevent the establishment of a standing army, the bane of liberty. Now, it must be evident, that, under this provision, together with their other powers, Congress could take such measures with respect to the militia, as to make a standing army necessary. Whenever Governments mean to invade the rights and liberties of the people, they always attempt to destroy the militia, in order to raise an army upon their ruins. This was actually done by Great Britain at the commencement of the late revolution. They used every means in their power to prevent the establishment of an effective militia to the eastward. The Assembly of Massachusetts, seeing the rapid progress that administration were making to divest them of their inherent privileges, endeavored to counteract them by the organization of the militia; but they were always defeated by the influence of the Crown."
- Rep. Elbridge Gerry of Massachusetts,
I Annals of Congress pg. 778, August 17, 1789[3]

"And that the said Constitution be never construed to authorize Congress to infringe the just liberty of the press, or the right of conscience; or to prevent the people of the United States, who are peaceable citizens, from keeping their own arms;"
- Motion added in the Massachusetts Convention (Debates of the Massachusetts Convention of 6 February 1788, p86)[4]

---

[2] Elliot, Jonathan. "Virginia Ratifying Convention." The Debates. Second ed. Vol. III. Washington: Congress, 1836. 47. Print.
Via <memory.loc.gov>

[3] Gales, Joseph, Sr. "House of Representatives, 1st Congress, 1st Session." The Debates and Proceedings of the Congress of the United States. Vol. 1. Washington: Gales and Seaton, 1834. 778. Print.
Via <memory.loc.gov>

[4] White, William. "Wednesday, February 6, 1788." *The Debates and Proceedings in the Convention of the Commonwealth of Massachusetts.* Boston: n.p., 1856. 86. Print.
Via <archive.org>

The bloody American Revolution was quite current in every Founder's mind. They could not so easily allow another tyrannical regime to obliterate the freedoms they so fervently fought and died to gain. Thus, they encouraged the writing of a Bill of Rights establishing the understanding that every citizen maintains various rights, one of which is the right to keep and bear arms.

In fact, prior to the writing of the Second Amendment, James Madison stated:

"The right of the people to keep and bear arms shall not be infringed; a well armed and well regulated militia being the best security of a free country..."

- *James Madison (Annals of Congress, pg. 451, 8 June 1789)*[5]

With this information, we can ascertain the Founders believed the People should have the means to defend themselves militarily from a tyrannical government independent of the standing army. It is the responsibility of the militia to defend freedom of oppression violently if necessary, naturally as a last resort.

---

[5] Gales, Joseph, Sr. "House of Representatives, 1st Congress, 1st Session." The Debates and Proceedings of the Congress of the United States. Vol. 1. Washington: Gales and Seaton, 1834. 451. Print.
Via <memory.loc.gov>

PART II
Dissecting the Second Amendment

A well-regulated Militia, being necessary to the security of a free State, the right of the people to keep and bear Arms, shall not be infringed.
-    *Second Amendment, Bill of Rights*

No amendment in the Bill of Rights or thereafter has created such divisive argument. The idea that common citizens, no matter their walk of life, can own as many or as few firearms as they please has been the subject of heated debate for years. On one side you have those who believe fully in the concept of the Second Amendment. On the other, there are those who see firearms as nothing but weapons of destruction. And of course there are plenty of gray area debaters to fill in the cracks.

Of late, the very meaning of the Second Amendment has come into question. Search the internet for the meaning behind this amendment and likely you will find various material saying this, that, or the other. Some will say it is for the militia only, and the National Guard is now that militia. Others will say it is for the people, who are the militia by default. And yet others will say the entire amendment is antiquated and should be removed altogether.

In order to put this debate to rest, we must dissect the Second Amendment in a way virtually never seen in any debate. To do so, we will break down the Second Amendment into four segments. The first segment is likely the most controversial. There are two key components encompassing much debate and battles of technicality. The most prominent of these components, of course, is the phrase "well regulated". Naturally, the modern anti-gun or even simply pro-gun control advocate will examine this phrase in its contemporary sense. The Merriam-Webster definition often used to describe "regulate" is such:

b. (1) to bring under the control of law or constituted authority (2) : to make regulations for or concerning

However, in the eighteenth century, the definition was slightly different. It is a small difference, but a considerable one. The Dictionary of the English Language by Samuel Johnson-1792 Edition defines "regulate":

1. To adjust by rule or method
2. To direct

There exists another word the Founders often coupled with "regulated". That word is "discipline". According to the same dictionary, "discipline" is defined:

6: a rule or system of rules governing conduct or activity

Of course, in the Second Amendment, the word regulated is accompanied by the word "well". The Samuel Johnson Dictionary defines "well":

3. Skillfully; properly
5. Not insufficiently; Not defectively

In conjunction with one another, "well regulated" can be seen as *skillfully or properly adjusted and directed by rule or method,* or *well disciplined.*

One might then say, "It is all about context." The one who says this would be correct. So let's see this term used in relation to the militia.

"The distinction between a well-regulated army and a mob, is the good order and discipline of the first, and the licentious and disorderly behaviour of the latter. Men, therefore, who are not employed as mere hirelings, but have stepped forth in defence of everything that is dear and valuable, not only to themselves but to posterity, should take uncommon pains to conduct themselves with uncommon propriety and good order, as their honour, reputation, &c., call loudly upon them for it."

Given under my hand, at Head Quarters, this 25th day of August, 1776.
GO˙ WASHINGTON.

- *George Washington (Orders to General Putnam 25 August 1776)[6]*

In his First Annual Address, Washington expanded on this idea:

"A free people ought not only to be armed, but disciplined; to which end, a uniform and well digested plan is requisite: and their safety and interest require that they should promote such manufactories as tend to render them independent on others for essential, particularly for military supplies."

- *George Washington (First Annual Message to Congress, 8 January 1790)[7]*

The second controversial word in the first part of the Second Amendment is "militia". Many modern Americans have a misunderstanding of what a militia is, especially in regard to what the Founding Fathers considered a "militia".

Through years of legislative changes and reinterpretations of Section 8 of the Constitution, the understanding of a militia and its use have become convoluted at best. Returning to the Constitution, Section 8 Clause 15 states:

---

[6] "Orders to Major General Israel Putnam, 25 August 1776," *Founders Online,* National Archives, last modified February 21, 2017, http://founders.archives.gov/documents/Washington/03-06-02-0113. [Original source: *The Papers of George Washington*, Revolutionary War Series, vol. 6, *13 August 1776–20 October 1776*, ed. Philander D. Chase and Frank E. Grizzard, Jr. Charlottesville: University Press of Virginia, 1994, pp. 126–128.]

[7] "From George Washington to the United States Senate and House of Representatives, 8 January 1790," *Founders Online,* National Archives, last modified February 21, 2017, http://founders.archives.gov/documents/Washington/05-04-02-0361. [Original source: *The Papers of George Washington*, Presidential Series, vol. 4, *8 September 1789–15 January 1790*, ed. Dorothy Twohig. Charlottesville: University Press of Virginia, 1993, pp. 543–549.]

To provide for organizing, arming, and disciplining, the militia, and for governing such part of them as may be employed in the service of the United States, reserving to the states respectively, the appointment of the officers, and the authority of training the militia according to the discipline prescribed by Congress;

Taking this Article at face value, many Americans believe the National Guard is the modern equivalent to the militia. Although there are some similarities, namely that the federal government "organizes, arms, and disciplines" the National Guard as it was commissioned to do with the Militia, there are important detail differences which divide them into two distinct entities. To determine this difference, one must take into account various documents: Constitution, Bill of Rights, Militia Act of 1792, Efficiency of Militia Bill (also known as the Dick Act of 1902), and the debates among the Founders.

The Constitution and Bill of Rights are the most common documents used regarding the understanding of a militia, but the Militia Act of 1792 clarifies who is required to enroll in the militia:

I. Be it enacted by the Senate and House of Representatives of the United States of America, in Congress assembled, That each and every free able-bodied white male citizen of the respective States, resident therein, who is or shall be of age of eighteen years, and under the age of forty-five years (except as is herein after excepted) shall severally and respectively be enrolled in the militia...

So what is the militia? This question which has been challenged almost exhaustively in the modern age. And it seems it was a question persistent in the 18th century as well. When the question arose during the debates over the ratification of the Constitution, George Mason had this to say:

"I ask, sir, what is the militia? It is the whole people, except for a few public officials."
>   -   *George Mason (Debates in Virginia Convention on Ratification of the Constitution, Elliot's Debates, Vol. 3, 16 June 1788)*[8]

Regarding the militia, in contrast with a National Guard type establishment, Richard Henry Lee, also known as the Federal Farmer, wrote:

"A militia, when properly formed, are in fact the people themselves, and render regular troops in a great measure unnecessary. The powers to form and arm the militia, to appoint their officers, and to command their services, are very important; nor ought they in a confederated republic to be lodged, solely, in any one member of the government. First, the constitution ought to secure a genuine and guard against a select militia, by providing that the militia shall always be kept well organized, armed, and disciplined, and include, according to the past and general usuage of the states, all men capable of bearing arms; and that all regulations tending to render this general militia useless and defenceless, by establishing select corps of militia, or distinct bodies of military men, not having permanent interests and attachments in the community to be avoided."

- *Richard Henry Lee (Federal Farmer, Letter XVIII, 25 January 1788)[9]*

These statements are important in that the militia is considered to be formed out of the people themselves. There was to be no Federal "select militia" contemporarily known as a National Guard. In fact, the definition of a militia as seen in the Dictionary of the English Language by Samuel Johnson -1792 Edition is such:

Militia:
1. The trainbands

Trainbands:
1. A part of the community trained to martial exercise

[8] Elliot, Jonathan. "Virginia Ratifying Convention." The Debates. Second ed. Vol. III. Washington: Congress, 1836. Print.

[9] Lee, Richard Henry. "Letters from the Federal Farmer, XVIII." Letter to The Republican. 25 Jan. 1788. *Lee Family Digital Archive.* N.p., n.d. Web. 24 Mar. 2017. <http://leefamilyarchive.org/papers/essays/fedfarmer/18.html>.

Notice the definition uses the word "community". The Minutemen of Lexington and Concord are perfect examples of "The trainbands". Furthermore, in addition to the statements given by various Founders and the literal definition, the Militia Act of 1792 established:

*That every citizen, so enrolled and notified, shall, within six months thereafter, **provide himself** (emphasis added) with a good musket or firelock, a sufficient bayonet and belt, two spare flints, and a knapsack, a pouch, with a box therein, to contain not less than twenty four cartridges, suited to the bore of his musket or firelock, each cartridge to contain a proper quantity of powder and ball; or with a good rifle, knapsack, shot-pouch, and powder-horn, twenty balls suited to the bore of his rifle, and a quarter of a pound of powder; and shall appear so armed, accoutred and provided, when called out to exercise or into service, except, that when called out on company days to exercise only, he may appear without a knapsack.*

This section is particularly noteworthy due to the fact it requires anyone enrolled in the Militia to provide their own firearms, ammunition, and equipment. It does not say the Federal Government will retain these firearms or equipment. The personal ownership of firearms and equipment is in line with yet another quote from Richard Henry Lee:

*"These corps, not much unlike regular troops, will ever produce an inattention to the general militia; and the consequence has ever been, and always must be, that the substantial men, having families and property, will generally be without arms, without knowing the use of them, and defenceless; **whereas, to preserve liberty, it is essential that the whole body of the people always possess arms, and be taught alike, especially when young, how to use them;**(emphasis added) nor does it follow from this, that all promiscuously must go into actual service on every occasion. **The mind that aims at a select militia, must be influenced by a truly anti-republican principle** (emphasis added); and when we see many men disposed to practice upon it, whenever they can prevail, no wonder true republicans are for carefully guarding against it. As a farther check, it may be proper to add, that the militia of any*

state shall not remain in the service of the union, beyond a given period, without the express consent of the state legislature." - Richard Henry Lee (Federal Farmer, Letter XVIII, 25 January 1788)[10]

Note: The term "republican" is not referring to the Republican Party, but rather a republican nation, more commonly referred to simply as a Republic.

The two emphasized portions of this statement are of paramount importance. The first makes it clear that each individual citizen has the right to own firearms for use in the preservation of liberty. The second discusses the detrimental fallacy in the creation of a "select militia", or in other terms, National Guard.

In the early days of the United States, it was considered a crucial and even honorable matter to ensure the People retained the instruments of their defense:

"The devising and establishing of a well regulated militia, would be a genuine source of legislative honor, and a perfect title to public gratitude. I, therefore, entertain a hope, that the present session will not pass, without carrying to its full energy the power of organizing, arming, and disciplining the militia; and thus providing, in the language of the constitution, for calling them forth to execute the laws of the union, suppress insurrections, and repel invasions."
- George Washington (Sixth Annual Message to Congress, 19 November 1794)[11]

---

[10] Lee, Richard Henry. "Letters from the Federal Farmer, XVIII." Letter to The Republican. 25 Jan. 1788. *Lee Family Digital Archive*. N.p., n.d. Web. 24 Mar. 2017. <http://leefamilyarchive.org/papers/essays/fedfarmer/18.html>.

[11] Washington, George. "Sixth Annual Message to Congress." 19 Nov. 1794. *Washington Papers*. Web. 24 Mar. 2017. <http://gwpapers.virginia.edu/documents/washingtons-sixth-annual-message-to-congress/>.

It will be prudent to pause here and take note of the recurring emphasis on discipline, not to be confused with control. During the American Revolution, particularly in its early days, there existed many problems among the state militias. George Washington often dealt with deserting militiamen and those who remained were often unruly. As the Commander in Chief, he felt he could not adequately rely on the militia in the rigors of war. This sentiment is often echoed among the other Founders when discussing the militia. The Founders not only wanted an armed populace, but one that could stand up to a trained and disciplined standing army. Here is part of a letter written by George Washington:

"The irregular and disjointed State of the Militia of this province, makes it necessary for me to inform you, that unless a Law is passed by your Legislature to reduce them to some order, and oblige them to turn out in a different Manner from what they have hitherto done, we shall bring very few into the Field, and even those few, will render little or no Service."
(This letter in its entirety can be found in Part IV)

This brings us to the Efficiency of Militia Bill. The primary reason for this bill was to give the Militia Act an "update" and create a more efficient system. Unfortunately, the concept became detrimental to the original intent of the Militia. The most resounding difference is seen here:

Sec. 13. That the Secretary of War is hereby authorized to issue, on the requisitions of the governors of the several States and Territories, or of the commanding general of the militia of the District of Columbia, such number of the United States service magazine rifles and carbines, with bayonets, bayonet scabbards, gun slings, web belts, and such other accouterments and equipments as are required for the Army of the United States, for arming all of the organized militia in said States and Territories and District of Columbia, without charging the same, or the cost or value thereof, against the allotment to said State, Territory, or District of Columbia, out of the annual appropriation provided by section sixteen hundred and sixty-one of the Revised Statutes, as amended, or requiring payment

"Let my beloved Americans guard against that fatal lethargy that has pervaded the universe. Have we the means of resisting disciplined armies, when our only defence, the militia, is put into the hands of Congress?"

- *Patrick Henry (3 Elliot's Debates 3:48, in Virginia Ratifying Convention)[13]*

Patrick Henry later added:

"Are we at last brought to such humiliating and debasing degradation, that we cannot be trusted with arms for our defense? Where is the difference between having our arms in possession and under our direction, and having them under the management of Congress? If our defense be the real object of having those arms, in whose hands can they be trusted with more propriety, or equal safety to us, as in our own hands?"

- *Patrick Henry (3 J. Elliot, Debates in the Several State Conventions pg. 168, 2d ed. Philadelphia, 1836)[14]*

The fact the Federal Government retains control over the firearms and equipment of the National Guard demonstrates it is but a shadow of its true intent. Unfortunately, the Efficiency of Militia Bill ushered in the demise of the traditional militia. Many states now forbid the establishment of an organized militia of any kind and view such organizations as terrorist in nature. It became the first step in the enslavement of the American People, even if the intentions were good.

After "militia", there is a break, a comma. Following this comma, is the phrase "*being necessary to the security of a free State*". A "State" is defined in the Samuel Johnson Dictionary as:

5. The community; the publick; the commonwealth
6. A republick; a government not monarchial

---

[13] Elliot, Jonathan. "Virginia Ratifying Convention." The Debates. Second ed. Vol. III. Washington: Congress, 1836. 48. Print.
Via <memory.loc.gov>

[14] Elliot, Jonathan. "Virginia Ratifying Convention." The Debates. Second ed. Vol. III. Washington: Congress, 1836. 168. Print.

therefor, and to exchange, without receiving any money credit therefor, ammunition, or parts thereof, suitable to the new arms, round for round, for corresponding ammunition suitable to the old arms theretofore issued to said State, Territory, or District by the United States: Provided, **_That said rifles and carbines and other property shall be receipted for and_** **_shall remain the property of the United States and be_** **_annually accounted for by the governors of the States and Territories_** *(emphasis added) as now required by law, and that each State, Territory, and District shall, on receipt of the new arms, turn in to the Ordnance Department of the United States Army, without receiving any money credit therefor, all United States rifles and carbines now in its possession.*

The concept of the government controlling the firearms was a notion to which many Founders were deeply opposed. The idea of government issued weapons and equipment were addressed during the Constitutional debates as seen here:

"An instance within memory of some of this house will show us how our militia may be destroyed. Forty years ago, when the resolution of enslaving America was formed in Great Britain, the British Parliament was advised by an artful man, who was governor of Pennsylvania, to disarm the people; that it was the best and most effectual way to enslave them; but that they should not do it openly, but weaken them, and let them sink gradually, by totally disusing and neglecting the militia. This was a most iniquitous project. Why should we not provide against the danger of having our militia, our real and natural strength, destroyed?"
- *George Mason (3 Elliot's Debates, pg 380, 14 June 1788)[12]*

---

[12] Elliot, Jonathan. "Virginia Ratifying Convention." The Debates. Second ed. Vol. III. Washington: Congress, 1836. 380. Print.

In the context of the Constitution, "State" refers to the former definition in relation to the latter; the public communities residing within a republic. Also take note it does not say Democracy.

Immediately succeeding this phrase are perhaps the most widely used, nearly to a fault, phrases:

"...the right of the people to keep and bear Arms, shall not be infringed."

Let us examine "right of the people to keep and bear arms" for a moment, beginning with their definitions. These are acutely important words within the Second Amendment since they establish the right for which we are fighting. Samuel Johnson's Dictionary defines:

> *Right:*
> 1. *Just claim*
> 2. *That which justly belongs to one*
> 3. *Property; interest*
> 4. *Power; prerogative*

> *People:*
> 1. *A nation; those who compose a community*

> *To Keep:*
>
> 1. *To retain; not to lose*
> 2. *To have in custody*
> 3. *To preserve; not to let go*

> *To Bear:*
> 1. *To carry as a burden*
> 2. *To convey or carry*
> 3. *To carry as a mark of authority*

> *Arms:*
> 1. *Weapons of offence, or armor of defense*

When one reads the definitions of these words it becomes remarkably transparent what the Founders were saying. This was not a shallow phrase they conjured up to satisfy a few loud representatives. It was by design the safeguard for all citizens and their communities. In fact, according to the definition of "arms", the Second Amendment extends not only to offensive weaponry, but defensive armor.

These phrases directly tie into the meaning of the militia in accordance with the Founders' understanding of the same. Seeing as a militia was considered the culmination of the People as a whole, it is only natural to assume the "right of the people" refers to all people within the republic and individual communities for use as a militia. This does not, however, stop at martial use. Keep in mind what Patrick Henry said, *"If our defense be the real object of having those arms, in whose hands can they be trusted with more propriety, or equal safety to us, as in our own hands?"*

The defense of one's self and family, and even community is at the heart of the Second Amendment. Self-defense is what drives it. And it is our natural right, or as the Declaration of Independence phrased it, "the separate and equal station to which the Laws of Nature and of Nature's God entitle them", to maintain the means of our defense. Defense against tyranny is only the most absolute version of self-defense.

Lastly, this right is solidified by the final phrase in the Second Amendment, "shall not be infringed." The definition of "infringe" is and remains:

1. To violate; to break laws or contracts
2. To destroy; to hinder

The Bill of Rights was written as a contract restricting the power of the government over the People. The Second Amendment was designed to secure that contract, in blood if need be, to safeguard the rights of all citizens of the United States. Many have proposed rewritings of the Second Amendment. Some of course are designed as a detriment to its intent, while others are an attempt at clarification.

However, if I were to rewrite the Second Amendment in a clarified form with respect to the context and definitions of each keyword, it may look something like this:

Amendment II: The whole people of the United States trained to martial exercise which is skillfully directed and properly disciplined and equipped, being necessary to the security of the community, the public, and the commonwealth of our Republic, the just claim and power of the whole nation, communities, and individuals to retain in custody and carry weapons of offence and armor of defense, shall not be violated, hindered, or destroyed.

Some would surmise the Second Amendment is "old fashioned" or irrelevant. Naturally, none of the other Amendments within the Bill of Rights are irrelevant, only the Second. I would declare the Second Amendment is just as relevant today, if not more so, as it was when it was penned. It is through the right of our defense that we can openly defy the decisions of the government and overturn that which we see as unconstitutional without fear of complete despotism. Yet, the Second retains its enemies.

There are a plethora of activists striving for nothing less than the destruction of the Second Amendment. Those who oppose the Second are not pressing for the abolition of the Third or Fourth Amendment. And of course, they can't call for the repeal of the First Amendment lest their efforts against the Second be silenced. One would be hard pressed to find someone who will say the right to free speech is antiquated, unless of course it is a modern "social justice warrior", but that is a different argument for another time. No logical citizen says you no longer have the right to privacy. No one is attempting to ban the Fifth Amendment. So why does there exist such a fervent attack on the Second Amendment?

My conclusion is the opponents of the Second Amendment, excluding politicians, have been drilled over and over with the perception that the need for guns would be unnecessary as long as the populace embraces a utopian way of life. This naturally sounds wonderfully blissful in theory. However, it ignores the human condition. The idea of a Utopia is nothing more than a pipe dream. A utopian society is simply dystopian despotism the citizens have unanimously decided to accept.

And in compound, there will always be someone who would prefer to hurt another rather than resolve matters peacefully. Worse still, there will always exist someone who will prey on the innocent for their own gain or satisfaction. These nefarious individuals are called criminals. They do not share in utopian desires. They do not adhere to the laws the good citizens choose to obey. If they did, they would not be criminals. For Utopia to exist, the world must first eradicate criminal activity, destroy evil, and create essentially autonomous "good" robots. There can be no free will in a true utopia. Utopian society requires a tight grip and careful thought control over its citizens lest they realize their enslavement.

Yet, so many citizens can't, or won't, see this illusive utopia as a negative concept. How could a world in which everyone peacefully coexists be wrong? It is not the result which is wrong, but the means. The means to a utopia is the destruction of many, the controlling of thought, and the strangling of freedom. Those who do not agree with the majority and could cause insurrection must be obliterated.

The human condition cannot be expelled. Even if all citizens agree to such an existence, eventually someone will take advantage of the good citizens of that society, whether it be a criminal or politician. And in said society, there would be no instrument, no device, and no means for the People to cast off their gilded chains.

People, for the most part, inherently want to be seen as good. In contrast, people are also capable of horrible and evil things. This combination creates the human condition. A good person can still become bad, just as a bad person can become good. Since there are those who would do wrong against others, the good people must have the means to defend and protect themselves and those they cherish. This has been understood since recorded history.

Now we are dealing with a mindset which states it is more moral to be a victim or to allow good people to die rather than to defend oneself. A woman attacked by a rapist should not defend herself lest she reduce herself to the attacker's "level". This is the argument. This is the mentality. This is simply wrong. All citizens, male and female, have the born right to defend themselves, by any means they so choose. For many, firearms are the most efficient tool for defense of life and family, whether from an attacker, a foreign enemy, or a tyrannical government. It serves as an equalizer. Who the aggressor is matters not, only that the defender has the best possible means of defense. And for this reason, the Second Amendment will forever be relevant.

PART IV

Additional Supporting Quotes and Documentation

Concerning the Militia

"But it ought always be held prominently in view that the safety of these States and of everything dear to a free people must depend in an eminent degree on the militia."
-James Monroe (First Inaugural Address, 1817)[15]

"It may be laid down as a primary position, and the basis of our system, that every Citizen who enjoys the protection of a free Government, owes not only a proportion of his property, but even of his personal services to the defence of it, and consequently that the Citizens of America (with a few legal and official exceptions) from 18 to 50 Years of Age should be borne on the Militia Rolls, provided with uniform Arms, and so far accustomed to the use of them, that the Total strength of the Country might be called forth at a Short Notice on any very interesting Emergency... "
- *George Washington (Article 1, Section 8, Clause 12, Sentiments on a Peace Establishment, 2 May 1783)[16]*

"The irregular and disjointed State of the Militia of this province, makes it necessary for me to inform you, that unless a Law is passed by your Legislature to reduce them to some order, and oblige them to turn out in a different Manner from what they have hitherto done, we shall bring very few into the Field, and even those few, will render little or no Service.

Their Officers are generally of the lowest Class of people, and instead of setting a good Example to their Men, are leading them into every kind of Mischief, one Species of which is, plundering the <u>Inhabitants under pretence of th</u>eir being Tories. A Law should in my

---

[15] Monroe, James. "First Inaugural Address." 4 Mar. 1817. *Yale Law School: Lillian Goldman Law Library*. Web. 24 Mar. 2017.
<http://avalon.law.yale.edu/19th_century/monroe1.asp>.

[16] Washington, George. "Sentiments on a Peace Establishment." Letter to Alexander Hamilton. 2 May 1783. *The Peace Establishment*. US Army, n.d. Web. 24 Mar. 2017.
<http://www.history.army.mil/books/RevWar/ss/peacedoc.htm>.

Opinion be passed, to put a stop to this kind of lawless Rapine, for unless there is something done to prevent it, the people will throw themselves of choice into the hands of the British Troops.

But your first object should be a well regulated Militia Law. The people, put under good Officers, would behave in quite another manner, and not only render real Service as Soldiers, but would protect, instead of distressing the Inhabitants.

What I would wish to have particularly insisted upon, in the new Law, should be, that every Man capable of bearing Arms, should be obliged to turn out, and not buy off their Service by a trifling Sum. We want Men and not Money. I have the Honor to be with the greatest Respect Sir Your most obt Servt"

- *George Washington (Letter to Governor William Livingston)*[17]

Disarming the Rebels at Concord

Lieut. Colonel Smith, 10th Regiment 'Foot,

Sir,

Having received intelligence, that a quantity of Ammunition, Provisions, Artillery, Tents and small Arms, have been collected at Concord, for the Avowed Purpose of raising and supporting a Rebellion against His Majesty, you will March with a Corps of Grenadiers and Light Infantry, put under your Command, with the utmost expedition and Secrecy to Concord, where you will seize and destroy all Artillery, Ammunition, Provisions, Tents, Small Arms, and all Military Stores whatever. But you will take care that the Soldiers do not plunder the Inhabitants, or hurt private property.

You have a Draught of Concord, on which is marked the Houses, Barns, &c, which contain the above military Stores. You will order a

[17] "From George Washington to William Livingston, 24 January 1777," *Founders Online*, National Archives, last modified February 21, 2017, http://founders.archives.gov/documents/Washington/03-08-02-0153. [Original source: *The Papers of George Washington*, Revolutionary War Series, vol. 8, *6 January 1777–27 March 1777*, ed. Frank E. Grizzard, Jr. Charlottesville: University Press of Virginia, 1998, pp. 147–148.]

Trunion to be knocked off each Gun, but if its found impracticable on any, they must be spiked, and the Carriages destroyed. The Powder and flower must be shook out of the Barrels into the River, the Tents burnt, Pork or Beef destroyed in the best way you can devise. And the Men may put Balls of lead in their pockets, throwing them by degrees into Ponds, Ditches &c., but no Quantity together, so that they may be recovered afterwards. If you meet any Brass Artillery, you will order their muzzles to be beat in so as to render them useless.

You will observe by the Draught that it will be necessary to secure the two Bridges as soon as possible, you will therefore Order a party of the best Marchers, to go on with expedition for the purpose.

A small party of Horseback is ordered out to stop all advice of your March getting to Concord before you, and a small number of Artillery go out in Chaises to wait for you on the road, with Sledge Hammers, Spikes, &c.

You will open your business and return with the Troops, as soon as possible, with I must leave to your own Judgment and Discretion.

I am, Sir,

Your   most   obedient   humble   servant Thos. Gage.[18]

[18] Gage, Thomas. "Orders to Lieut. Colonel Smith, 10th Regiment 'Foot." Letter to LTC. Smith. 18 Apr. 1775. *TeachingAmericanHistory.org*. N.p., n.d. Web. 24 Mar. 2017. <http://teachingamericanhistory.org/library/document/orders-from-general-thomas-gage-to-lieut-colonel-smith-10th-regiment-foot/>.

Defending Against Tyranny

"And what country can preserve its liberties, if its rulers are not warned from time to time, that its people preserve the spirit of resistance? Let them take arms...The tree of liberty must be refreshed from time to time, with the blood of patriots and tyrants."
- Thomas Jefferson Letter to William S. Smith 13 Nov 1787 [19]

"If the representatives of the people betray their constituents, there is then no recourse left but in the exertion of that original right of self-defense which is paramount to all positive forms of government, and which against the usurpations of the national rulers may be exerted with infinitely better prospect of success than against those of the rulers of an individual State. In a single State, if the persons entrusted with supreme power become usurpers, the different parcels, subdivisions, or districts of which it consists, having no distinct government in each, can take no regular measures for defense. The citizens must rush tumultuously to arms, without concert, without system, without resource; except in their courage and despair."
-Alexander Hamilton (Federalist No. 28) [20]

[19] *"From Thomas Jefferson to William Stephens Smith, 13 November 1787," Founders Online, National Archives, last modified December 28, 2016, http://founders.archives.gov/documents/Jefferson/01-12-02-0348. [Original source: The Papers of Thomas Jefferson, vol. 12, 7 August 1787–31 March 1788, ed. Julian P. Boyd. Princeton: Princeton University Press, 1955, pp. 355–357.]*

[20] Hamilton, Alexander. "Federalist No. 28." The Federalist Papers: A Collection of Essays Written in Support of the Constitution of the United States from the Original Text of Alexander Hamilton, James Madison and John Jay. 2nd ed. Baltimore: Johns Hopkins UP, 1986. N. pag. Print.

PART V
Quotes Not to Use

There are many spurious quotes floating in the sea of misinformation that is the internet. Especially of late, many quotes have been wrongly attributed to various Founding Fathers. Some seem to be improper paraphrases while others are completely fabricated or failing in context. Using such quotes in your arguments will only hurt your case and render you perceived as ignorant.

"A free people ought not only be armed and disciplined, but they should have sufficient arms and ammunition to maintain a status of independence from any who might attempt to abuse them, which would include their own government."
- George Washington

This is a quote that is only partially correct. However, most of it is wrong in both language and context. The real quote has been annotated in this book.

"No freeman shall ever be debarred the use of arms."
-Thomas Jefferson

Although this is something that is rightly attributed to Mr. Jefferson, the context is often skewed. It is important to take note that this was part of the first of three drafts written for the Virginia Constitution. No version or variant thereof was adopted in the final draft.[21]

---

[21] "Thomas Jefferson's Monticello." *No Freeman Shall Be Debarred the Use of Arms (Spurious Quotation) | Thomas Jefferson's Monticello.* N.p., n.d. Web. 24 Mar. 2017. <https://www.monticello.org/site/jefferson/no-freeman-shall-be-debarred-use-arms-spurious-quotation>.

"The thoughtful reader may wonder, why wasn't Jefferson's proposal of 'No freeman shall ever be debarred the use of arms' adopted by the Virginia legislature? They that can give up essential liberty to obtain a little temporary safety deserve neither liberty nor safety."
- Benjamin Franklin

It is well known that the latter sentence of this quote was certainly written by Benjamin Franklin in his book *Historical Review of Pennsylvania* published in 1759. However, none of the wording prior exists within the pages of this work.

"To disarm the people is the most effectual way to enslave them."
- George Mason

Technically speaking, George Mason said this. However, it is a paraphrase of something he actually said. He was referencing what the Governor of Pennsylvania told the King of England while advising him on how to subdue the colonials. The true quote has been annotated in this book.

PART VI
Arguments Against the Second Amendment and Gun Ownership
(and How to Reply to Them)

There are numerous common, and obscure, arguments which anti-gun advocates attempt to use to justify either strict gun laws or an all-out gun ban. Most have already been indirectly addressed in the first part of this book. In this section I will offer other arguments and how to reply. Every one listed is an argument against which I've had to defend.

Argument 1: The Founding Fathers would not have written the Second Amendment if they knew how much the firearm would advance.

Reply: The Founders had already seen vast improvements of the firearm. From multi-barreled pistols to advancements in firing systems. They saw the evolution from stick to primer, to Matchlock, to Wheel Lock, to Flintlock. During the age of Enlightenment, the Founders, and all thinking men of that era were looking to the future and its advancements. This included advancements in firearms.

In regard to same, in 1718 James Puckle invented the predecessor to the Gatling Gun. This was the first true attempt at a repeating "machinegun". He called it the Defence Gun, contemporarily known as the Puckle Gun. Unfortunately, the Flintlock technology was far too unreliable to be implemented on the battlefield.[22] The one piece of the puzzle which hindered the advancement of firearms was the self-contained cartridge. If the self-contained cartridge had been invented earlier in history, we could very well have seen the invention of repeating firearms a hundred years before their real world rise.

Additionally, it is good to note that although powder based firearms were slow in advancements, the air guns of the 18th century

---

[22] "The Machine Gun's Grandpa: The Puckle Gun." *Oddly Historical*. N.p., 25 Feb. 2015. Web. 25 Mar. 2017. <http://www.oddlyhistorical.com/2014/05/12/machine-guns-grandpa-puckle-gun/>.

were similar to the modern firearms we see today. For instance, the Girandoni Air Rifle, invented by Bartolomeo Girandoni around 1778 was used by the Lewis and Clark Expedition. This rifle was a .46 caliber, magazine fed, rifle with an effective range of 150 yards with a magazine capacity of 22 rounds. This rifle would technically be illegal in states such as New York or California if the Air Gun had replaced the powder based firearms. Although they never replaced powder based firearms, Big Bore Air Rifles still exist and are used in big game hunting.

__Argument 2:__ People don't need firearms because it is so rare to ever need one. (This argument is often accompanied by statistics of varying information)

__Reply:__ The largest flaw to this argument is that it ignores the people have been in situations where they needed a firearm. The notion that since not everyone needs one, then no one needs one, is fundamentally asinine. According to the National Safety Council, you have a 1 in 9,821 chance of dying in an air and space transport incident[23]. Yet, every plane has seat belts, floatation devices, emergency evacuation equipment, and puts their passengers through a safety brief regarding what to do in case such an event occurs.

In contrast, according to the National Safety Council, the chances of being assaulted with a firearm is 1 in 370[24]. So by the statistics, it stands within reasonable possibility that you could end up in an altercation in which you need to defend yourself. And a firearm is the most efficient and equalizing means to establish that defense. One is only unlikely to be attacked with a firearm, until they are attacked with a firearm. When that happens, 1 in 370 becomes 1 in 1. At that moment, statistics, gun laws, legislation, morality, are all for naught.

---

[23] "What Are the Odds of Dying From..." *National Safety Council.* N.p., n.d. Web. 24 Mar. 2017. <http://www.nsc.org/learn/safety-knowledge/Pages/injury-facts-chart.aspx>

[24] "What Are the Odds of Dying From..." *National Safety Council.* N.p., n.d. Web. 24 Mar. 2017. <http://www.nsc.org/learn/safety-knowledge/Pages/injury-facts-chart.aspx>

Argument 3: Why does anyone need a 30 round magazine (typically clip for the uninformed) to hunt a deer? Variations include assault rifle in place of 30 round magazine.

Reply (30 round magazine): Bring them back to the purpose of the Second Amendment and Patrick Henry's arguments. The reason harkens back to the concept of the trainbands. We as citizens have the right to defend ourselves in the best possible way, whether defending against a criminal or a tyrannical government. Now, a 30 round magazine may not be an everyday carry item, but if the need should arise, you will have it.

Reply (Assault Weapon): This is an argument on semantics. Since it is a bit more ambiguous, I will give you tips on how to reply to it rather than an actual reply.

You must first establish what they consider an Assault Weapon. This is where they may use the "30 round magazine" and other cosmetic features in their assessment. Once the definition has been established, discuss the flaws in thinking regarding firearms. For instance, having a telescoping buttstock does not make the firearm more deadly, nor does more ammunition in the magazine. The person's intent is what makes a firearm dangerous, not the firearm itself.

You can discuss the percentage of "Assault Weapons" used in crime in relation to pistols. Use sources such as the CDC or other government entities. Do NOT use Fox News, the NRA, or other conservative/libertarian sources. Although these can be legitimate sources, they will be quickly dismissed as propaganda and will hurt your argument. This is good advice for any argument concerning the Second Amendment.

Argument 4: You are indirectly responsible for every death by firearm in the United States because you are pro-gun.

Reply: A gun owner is no more responsible for the actions of other gun owners, either direct or indirect, than a car owner is responsible for the actions of another car owner. This is true of everything any mass amount of the population collectively owns. This argument removes personal responsibility and morality and places the blame onto the ownership of an object. "Because you own x, you are responsible for what other x owners do with x". If one were to use this argument in regard to anything else, they would be viewed as a buffoon and quickly dismissed as an illogical person.

Argument 5: In "X" country you can buy an AK-47 for $100, yet there was still a mass shooting and no one stopped it.

Reply: When I was confronted with this argument, I had to do some research. The country in question turned out to have (1) strict gun laws, (2) was essentially run by militant gangs, and (3) had a considerable poor population. If confronted with such an argument, do your research concerning whatever country is being discussed. In this instance, yes, one could buy an AK-47 for $100 USD. However, for the general population, not only did the government restrict the purchase of such a weapon, that $100 might as well have been $10,000 due to their economic state. Just because a firearm can be purchased for cheap it does not mean everyone in that country has one, or can acquire one.

Argument 6: Any citizen who purchases a firearm should be mandated to attend a training session on the use of that firearm.

Reply: Although on the surface this seems to be a good idea, it creates two issues. The first is the likelihood of a registration process. The second, whenever the government mandates something for the citizens, a fee is usually involved. A citizen should not be required to (1) register a firearm with the government, nor (2) pay the government additional fees to retain their property. However, I do believe training should be offered to the citizens by the government free of charge. Provided training is a constitutionally sound concept.

Argument 7: The government won't take advantage of a firearm registration database.

Reply: The government has already taken advantage of such a thing. Recent events such as California's recent firearms ban[25] reveal this idea to be false. Confiscation can also be seen in other pro-gun control countries such as Canada. And how do these governments know who has firearms? Registration databases. So the notion that the government wouldn't take advantage of such a database has already been debunked, by the actions of existing governments.

Argument 8: Less guns means less violence.

Reply: Violence is not reliant on the tools of its execution. Violence is within the heart and mind of the person committing the violent act. Banning guns will not eradicate violence, only violence with that tool. And along that same vein, those who do not adhere to the rule of law will still use guns in their nefarious endeavors. Those who are evil will continue to be evil unless a change in heart and mind occurs, not because an inanimate object is removed.

Argument 9: It would be impossible to fight the current standing army with only civilian firearms, so why bother?

Reply: Both historical and recent wars point out various flaws in this logic. One such flaw pertains to the overall point of the argument, that the standing army would crush any rebellion.

[25] Elinson, Zusha. "New California Law Lowers the Bar for Gun Seizures." *The Wall Street Journal.* Dow Jones & Company, 02 July 2016. Web. 25 Mar. 2017. <https://www.wsj.com/articles/new-california-law-lowers-the-bar-for-gun-seizures-1467409616>.

In both the Revolutionary War and the Civil War we witnessed a split within the military. During the American Revolution, the colonials were divided into the Patriots and the Loyalists. Both these factions became their own standing armies, either through militia or by joining the Continental Army or the British Army.

In the Civil war, many officers and enlisted, such as Robert E. Lee and Thomas "Stonewall" Jackson, within the Federal Army deserted and joined the Confederate Army, taking with them the equipment and knowledge of their former order. In the modern age, this would likely happen again. So we would not have to fight with only the basic firearms our masters allow.

Furthermore, one only need to observe the tactics employed by various "inferior" forces, such as the Viet Cong, Taliban, and Iraqi Insurgency. Even an inferior force can disrupt a larger entity. In the same manner, the American people know their land and how to use it should such a horrendous event as a second civil war should occur. God forbid it!

PART VII
Tips for Debating the Second Amendment, Gun Ownership, and Other Debates

Tip 1. When discussing what the Founding Fathers believed about the right to keep and bear arms, use sources from the 18th century. Do not use modern articles that comment on what the Founders believed. Go directly to the documents, whether it be letters, annals, or dictionaries. Your argument will be more accurate and definitive if you do a little additional research to find the actual quotes of the Founders. There are plenty of accessible information through the internet in this regard. Many official archives, such as the Library of Congress and the National Archives, have put these documents into digital form on their websites.

Tip 2. When using statistics, utilize government sources such as the CDC, NSC, FBI, &c. Additionally, if you decide to use a news article, use a news source that your opponent may attempt to use against you. For example, in the second argument, I used CNN as one of the sources. Many anti-gun advocates trust CNN, so it will support your argument further as opposed to a news source they consider "untrustworthy". Know thy enemy, so to speak.

Tip 3. DO NOT revert to insults. Once insults are introduced into the argument there will no longer be logical conversation. Your opponent may be as dumb as a box of rocks, but treat them as if they are your intellectual superior.

Tip 4. When you find common ground with your opponent, take advantage of it. Use this time to discuss important issues in which you and they may agree. This will do two things. It will create an understanding between the two of you and reduce tensions which may lead to insult. As it was sang in Boston following the ratification of the Constitution:

Now politicians of all kinds,
Who are not yet decided,
May see how Yankees speak their minds,
And yet are not divided.

Tip 5. DO NOT, I say again, DO NOT use "Meme University" for your quotes. There are far too many "quotes", which the Founders never said, floating in image form throughout the vastness of the internet. I implore you to look up the quote and verify. If you find that it is false, then search for the real quote. Once you find the real quote, document the source, both original and the internet source. This will save you embarrassment and humiliation in the future.

Tip 6: Remember, context is key. Try not to dice up a quote. This is done by so many debaters. They cherry pick quotes without giving the proper context. As mentioned earlier, this can be seen with the majority of pro-Second Amendment advocates when they only use "the right of the people to keep and bear Arms, shall not be infringed". Although this is not necessarily bad, it often evokes an aura of ignorance. Do not be afraid to use a quote or section of the Constitution in its entirety. And on the same note, be sure you understand the wording and context of everything you use.

Tip 7: When quoting a Founder, do not simply say, "X Founder said thus." Include where and when they said it. This drives the message home and establishes that you understand the subject matter of which you are debating. This misstep is perhaps the most prolific reason "Meme University" exists.

Tip 8: When discussing the use of deadly force as a means of self-defense in a debate, do not speak of it in a cavalier way. It is a serious matter and should be treated as such. The opposition already considers many pro-gun advocates to be "wannabe cowboys" or "war mongers". Do not prove them right with the language you use regarding defending your life. Remember, the person you are